Also by Jim Prime

From Moose House Publications

- *Fish and Dicks*: Case files from the Digby Neck and Islands Fish-Gutting Service and Detective Agency
- *Beyond the Passage*: short stories from Long Island, NS

Some of Jim's other books

Ted Williams Hit List (with Ted Williams)
Tales from the Boston Red Sox Dugout
More Tales from the Boston Red Sox Dugout
The Little Red (Sox) Book (with Bill Lee)
Red Sox Essentials
Baseball Eccentrics (with Bill Lee)
How Hockey Explains Canada (with Paul Henderson)
The Goal that United Canada
Amazing Tales from the 2004 Boston Red Sox Dugout
Ted Williams: a Tribute
Ted Williams: a Splendid Life
Fenway Park at 100
Fenway Saved

Tales from the Toronto Blue Jays Dugout
The Boston Red Sox World Series Encyclopedia
From the Babe to the Beards
Ted Williams, the Pursuit of Perfection
The Barber of Mud Creek
Boston Red Sox Killer Bs: Baseball's Best Outfield

ICE DREAMS

The
1972
SUMMIT SERIES,
50 years on

Jim Prime

foreword by
Ron Ellis

illustrations by
Catherine Prime

Cover image: Catherine Prime
Editor: Andrew Wetmore
ISBN: 978-1-990187-51-3
First edition November 2022

MOOSE HOUSE
PUBLICATIONS

2475 Perotte Road
Annapolis County, NS
B0S 1A0

moosehousepress.com
info@moosehousepress.com

We live and work in Mi'kma'ki, the ancestral and unceded territory of the Mi'kmaw People. This territory is covered by the "Treaties of Peace and Friendship" which Mi'kmaw and Wolastoqiyik (Maliseet) People first signed with the British Crown in 1725. The treaties did not deal with surrender of lands and resources but in fact recognized Mi'kmaq and Wolastoqiyik (Maliseet) title and established the rules for what was to be an ongoing relationship between nations. We are all Treaty people.

Foreword

On September 28, 2022, I was able to celebrate a lifetime experience with my teammates on Team Canada '72'. The date marks the 50th anniversary of Team Canada's victory over the Soviet Union in the Summit Series that would once and for all determine which country would be the number one hockey power in the world.

Hockey fans remember the Paul Henderson goal that gave us the win with 34 seconds left in the 3rd period of game 8. They also remember the obstacles we had to overcome, the adversity we had to face and the resilience we had to show throughout the series to give us victory.

Ron Ellis in the 1967 Stanley Cup parade, the last year the Toronto Maple Leafs captured the cup

Jim Prime wrote this book geared to the younger generation to help them understand the importance the Summit Series played in Canadian hockey history and the impact it had on Canadian culture. I also believe he wrote the book to encourage young people facing challenges today to believe they can indeed achieve their goals in life.

My Ice Dream to become a NHL hockey player started when I was about 10 years old. At the time, I was playing minor hockey and enjoying the game I loved with my friends but I was not the best player on the ice. I had an obstacle, a physical limitation that left me with 70% forward flexibility in my left ankle.

Getting to the next level would not be an easy journey but with the support of my parents and a favourite teacher I pressed on.

Over time, with a lot of hard work adapting my skating stride and developing other hockey skills my game came together.

By the time I was 15 years old, I was playing junior hockey with the Toronto Marlies, who were owned by the Toronto Maple Leafs. After we won the Memorial Cup in 1964, the Leafs signed me to a professional contract. Can you imagine how I felt the first time I pulled a Toronto Maple Leaf jersey over my head?

Life is difficult but that doesn't mean we shouldn't have dreams about becoming an athlete, a teacher, a doctor or a computer programmer. Everyone who has a dream of a worthy goal will face obstacles such as bullying, poverty, prejudice and worry. If you find yourself in this situation, surround yourself with good people who believe in you and want to support you on your personal journey.

Now is the time to start the hard work and be prepared to fight through adversity with a never give up attitude.

Team Canada '72' never gave up!

Ron Ellis
October 2022

to Paul, Ron, Bobby and Serge
and all the members of Team Canada,
and to all those young men and women who work to overcome life's
challenges in pursuit of their dreams, hockey or otherwise.

The author, like most Canadians alive at that time, followed the Summit Series closely. Since then, he has written about it, interviewed participants, and analyzed the effect of the Series on the spirit of Canada. Here he tells the story from his point of view. Any errors or omissions are not intentional.

Ice Dreams

1: Ice dreams

They came together from villages, towns, and cities across Canada. Some lived in isolated mining communities, others in high rise apartments. Some grew up in families that had lived here for many generations. Others were the sons and grandsons of immigrants who had come to Canada to find a better life.

The one thing they had in common was their love of hockey. They learned the game by playing with their brothers and sisters and friends. They played it every chance they got. They played it in their basements, using a rolled-up sock as a puck. Or in the driveway or road using boots as goalposts.

They learned to skate on backyard rinks or nearby ponds. They listened to NHL games on radio or watched them on TV. A few of the lucky ones even got to watch them in person.

The more they played the better they got. They loved to test themselves against their friends and learn new things: how to deke out a defenseman, how to shoot the puck, how to make a pass, how to make a save.

As they played, they pretended to be their favourite NHL hero and copied his style. Many dreamed of someday playing for their favourite NHL team. They pictured themselves scoring the game-winning goal or making the key save in Game Seven of the Stanley Cup finals. They imagined skating around the ice lifting the gleaming Cup high over their heads as the hometown crowd went wild. Or having an Olympic gold medal hung around their neck as *O Canada* was being played.

For most of us, things like this remain just dreams, but for these boys the future unfolded to reveal a reality that was beyond even their wildest dreams.

When they were still boys, the future members of Team Canada had no way of knowing that their love of the game would bring them together to play for Canada in the most famous hockey series in our history.

~

One of those boys was **Bobby Clarke**. Bobby grew up in Flin Flon, a mining town in northern Manitoba. His father worked in the mines and most of his friends were the sons of miners.

The winters in northern Manitoba are six or seven months long and brutally cold. His dad made a rink in the backyard. That's where he got hooked on hockey. He took to ice like a duck to water.

"I started playing hockey when I was two years old on the outdoor ice," Bobby says. "Every kid I knew played hockey, and in the summer we played street hockey. Hockey was the main, consistent ingredient in our growing up."

As he grew, his love of the game grew with him. He began playing organized hockey when he was eight years old. Each year he got stronger and faster. Soon he was the best player on his team.

Then, when he was 12 years old, his whole world seemed to come crashing down. He noticed that he was thirsty all the time and that he was losing weight no matter how much he ate. His mom took him to the doctor, who told him he had type 1 diabetes. Type 1 diabetes is a disease that can sap your energy and affect your vision. There is also the danger of seizures. Bobby was afraid that he might not be able to play hockey any more.

A diabetes specialist told him he could play if he followed his instructions closely. He had to watch his diet and get regular insulin injections.

Bobby tried his best to follow the doctor's orders, but continued to get up before dawn to skate in the backyard until it was time to go to school.

He was embarrassed about his diabetes. Too ashamed to tell his friends about it. He thought it made him different. He didn't want to be singled out and called a "diabetic athlete." He was a hockey player who happened to have diabetes.

Each day when school was over, he hit the ice with his buddies. "You knew everyone in your neighbourhood," he says. "Everybody was friends, all the kids up and down the street."

Darkness came early in this northern mining town.

"Flin Flon days were shorter. I don't have any idea why I wanted to get on the ice at 5 in the morning before school when the outdoor ice had just been flooded. It was really cold. I don't know why I wanted to stay out after dark playing... until my mom got really mad at me. I have no idea why the game had such a grasp on me."

The Clarke family didn't own a TV but Bobby didn't mind. He listened to NHL games on the radio.

"I was 14 by the time we got TV. When it got really cold outside, some of the kids kind of faded away and got into TV. I never did. I just wanted to play hockey."

Bobby's goal was to play for the hometown Flin Flon Bombers, and when he was 17 he made the team. NHL scouts came to watch him play. They were impressed with his talent and hard work. Until they heard about his diabetes. Then most of them stopped coming. They thought that type 1 diabetes meant that he wasn't tough enough to play pro hockey.

Bobby was determined to prove them wrong. "I didn't need diabetes to motivate me, though. I didn't feel resentment about it. I just wanted to get on the ice and show that I could play. I had an attitude. I think the geography of the West makes you tougher. We played a tougher style. Even if we weren't tougher, we thought we were."

Only one NHL scout continued to believe in him. He convinced the Philadelphia Flyers to take a chance. Against all odds, Bobby Clarke became the first NHL star with diabetes—and the first to become a team captain.

~

Further east, in the small town of Lucknow, Ontario, **Paul Henderson** didn't learn to skate until he was nine years old because his parents couldn't afford to buy him skates. Paul wasn't going to let that stop him from playing hockey.

"It all started with road and floor hockey," Paul says. "That's when I got a taste of what the game's all about. I went to Cub Scouts and Boy Scouts mainly to play floor hockey. I couldn't wait to get a-hold of a stick and play. It was just such a wonderful sport."

Even without skates, he managed to learn the game well.

"We lived next door to the Chan family. They owned the only Chinese restaurant in town. They had seven sons who were all great hockey players. One was my own age. They invited me over to play ball hockey in their basement. I didn't even have a hockey stick but they let me use one of theirs."

When Paul turned nine he finally got his first pair of skates. He was itching to try them out on real ice.

"They were second-hand and I remember I had four pairs of socks in them because they were so big. At first my shin pads were old Eaton's catalogues stuffed into my pant legs and held in place by strong elastic bands. Then the Chans gave me their old gloves and shin pads. The gloves had holes, but that was okay."

There was no artificial ice in Lucknow. Paul practised skating on neighbourhood ponds and soon discovered that he was fast on blades. Very fast. Faster than any of his friends. His speed made him almost unstoppable as he zoomed past opposing defensemen.

"I had a passion for hockey that surprised even me," he says. "When I started to play the game on ice I had trouble sleeping the night before a game. And then I'd go to school and have trouble concentrating on the classes. I was always thinking, 'Oh, we're going to play hockey tonight.' I was fast, I was good, I was strong, and I could dominate.

"Growing up, all my heroes were hockey players. My dad and I listened to Foster Hewitt announce the Maple Leaf games on the radio. At first my favourite player was Gordie Howe and then it became Jean Beliveau."

Even as a young boy, Paul saw hockey as a way to lift his family out of poverty.

"I hated being poor. The lack of money caused great stress for my whole family. I vowed that I would never live like this. I wanted to be financially secure. I loved to play hockey and I knew that professional hockey players got paid lots of money. My ultimate dream was to be an NHL player. The idea of playing against my NHL heroes made me try harder. I wanted to make a living doing something I loved, and that was hockey. I wanted to look forward to going to work each day."

At a peewee tournament in nearby Goderich, Paul scored six goals in one game. People were starting to notice him. Other teams were doing everything to try to stop him. Because Lucknow was so small he ended up playing with and against much older, and much bigger, players. This forced him to develop his other hockey skills.

"I soon found out that nothing comes easy. Guys who are successful are successful for a reason. I knew I had to be prepared to work hard if I was going to make it to the NHL. The farther you move up the competitive ladder, the better you have to be. There was no hockey school so I had to do it myself.

"But I never forgot to have fun. You have to enjoy the game. As soon as you start putting pressure on yourself and trying to do things you can't do you're in trouble. You have to know your strengths."

By the time he turned 15, Paul could skate like the wind. Minor league scouts started showing up at his games, scribbling furiously in their notebooks as his goals started to pile up. He learned to deke out an opponent and perfected his wrist shot—mainly because he was afraid of breaking his stick on slap shots. After all, sticks were expensive.

He really got everyone's attention when he scored 18 goals. Not a bad season total, you say? Well, those 18 goals came in a single game, as he led

Lucknow to a 21-6 win over Wainfleet.

When Paul was born on January 28, 1943, his father, Garnet, was away in Europe, fighting in World War II. In fact, Paul didn't even meet his dad until he was three years old. Garnet had been wounded in battle but never talked about it.

As he grew up, Paul found it difficult to talk to his dad about anything. At times Garnet could be very hard on his son, especially when it came to hockey. No matter how many goals Paul scored, it seemed that his dad was never happy.

"Dad always had a hard time expressing his feelings to me. I had three younger sisters and dad used to say to them, 'Your dad really loves you.' I can't remember him ever saying that to me."

Garnet Henderson coached Paul's peewee team. One time in the dressing room between periods, he spoke to the players and said, "Just give the puck to Paul and get out of the way. He'll score for you." Paul's heart sank. He hated being singled out like that.

"I still remember that night like it was yesterday," says Paul. "I was so embarrassed I couldn't even look up. I thought, *Dad how could you ever do that to me?*"

During the drive home from the game, Paul was quiet, staring straight ahead. "I wanted to cry. Then suddenly a smile came to my face. I looked out the window of the car and I thought, *My father thinks I'm really good. My father thinks I'm better than the whole team.* And I felt better. You look back over your life and you realize how significant that was. That was why I had such confidence. Now I realized how proud he was of me. My dad thinks I'm really good. He must love me *too.*

"Later, when I became a dad myself, I learned that a father needs to let his children know three things: that he loves them, that he's proud of them, and that they are *good* at something.

"Everyone has talents. In my case I was a good athlete and played every sport. I was a really good hockey player. I always had self-confidence and I was always very competitive no matter what game I played. I knew I was good. If you play tiddly winks with me, I'm going to try to beat you."

Before long pro scouts from Toronto, Detroit and Boston travelled to Lucknow to check out the rising star. Soon the Detroit Red Wings made an offer that Paul liked, and the 16-year old prospect signed a contract with their Junior B team. At first he was happy but as time passed in the minors he realized that the road to the NHL would be long and difficult. He was at a turning point.

"I was going to quit because I knew it was a long shot to make an NHL team. I told my dad I was quitting.

"He said, 'Son, for years you've told all your friends you're going to be an NHL hockey player and I think when you see those guys skate out on the ice on Saturday night, you're going to sit there and wonder if you could have made it. I think it will drive you crazy.' It was such great advice. He encouraged me, he didn't force me. I decided to keep playing.

"What if I had quit? Can you imagine the life I would have missed if I had hadn't become an NHL player? I've travelled the world and visited over 50 countries because of hockey. **My dad was right.** Sometimes I used to get ticked off with my parents because we had no money at all. Now I thank God for them all the time."

~

Ronnie Ellis grew up in the town of Lindsay, Ontario, near Toronto. His father had played professional hockey in the American Hockey League. "I was a hockey kid, born and bred," he says. "I had the game in my family and in my blood. My dream was to be a Leaf." With his dad as his minor hockey coach, he worked hard to make that happen. But before that could happen there were problems to overcome.

"I was born with a club foot. My left foot was turned inward and down," he says. "I had to wear a brace on it and my mom took me to Sick Kids Hospital in Toronto once a month for treatment."

The brace was working but he was five years old before it was finally removed. His foot was now straight but his left ankle had lost a lot of strength. It was much weaker than his right and there was little flexibility. He was determined not to let it stop him from playing hockey.

"That was my challenge," he says.

His father came up with a plan. "I had a little red wagon. To strengthen my left leg, my dad built a little wall on the right hand side so I could only put my right leg in and push with my left ankle."

The plan helped but his left ankle would always be weaker.

"I was eight years old before I could play minor hockey. Skating was my strength and I was fast. I could skate in a straight line very well but I had trouble cutting to the net from the left side because my ankle was weak. I was much stronger cutting to the net from the right side. I was a right hand shot. I had to adapt."

Like Bobby Clarke, Ronnie didn't tell friends about his problem. He didn't want to use his club foot as an excuse. "Hockey players are real people with real problems," he says.

Instead, he worked hard to improve. He skated and skated and skated and before long he was the fastest kid on the ice.

"Dad had been an exceptional player. Mom kept his scrapbooks and many times I'd look through them and think, 'Wow!' They gave me the incentive to get better. I dreamed about playing hockey like my dad. I thought, 'Hey maybe I can do that too.'

"My dad knew my dream was to play pro hockey and he always

encouraged me. Sometimes I'd get frustrated and want to quit. There were times when he had to be a little tough on me to keep me going. He didn't let me quit. He knew I had the ability and kept me on the road to help my dream come true. Parents are sometimes in a difficult position between being encouraging and being forceful."

"I knew I had to work harder to accomplish my goals. I didn't want people to know about my foot. I kept it to myself because I thought teams might not want to take a chance on me. I adapted my skating style. Sometimes in life you have to adapt to overcome your challenges. That's what I've learned. Sometimes those challenges are physical ones and sometimes they are something else."

Ronnie was a good student, but school was difficult because he also had a speech impediment. He worked hard to overcome it. Hockey allowed him to forget his problems for a while and just play.

"I always felt a sense of freedom on the ice, away from everything. It's one of the reasons I love the game. Hockey saved me. I was able to excel on the ice. I felt accepted."

All the hard work and perseverance paid off when Maple Leaf scouts came to visit Ronnie's parents when he was 14. The next year he joined the Toronto Marlboros. When he was still in school, he got a one-game call-up to play for Toronto against the Montreal Canadiens. He didn't bother to tell his schoolmates because he thought he'd just be sitting on the bench.

Imagine his friends' surprise when they tuned in to watch the game that night and there was Ronnie playing on a line with superstar Frank Mahovlich. He played the whole game as the Leafs beat the Habs 1-0.

Ronnie played his first season with Toronto in 1964-65 and in 1966-67 the kid with a club foot skated around the ice with the Stanley Cup held high. It was the last time the Toronto Maple Leafs would win the Cup for at least 55 years.

~

Serge Savard grew up in Landrienne, a hotbed of hockey, 400 miles northwest of Montreal in northern Quebec. "It was a very small village," he says. "We played on outside rinks because that was the only ice. We had to do everything for ourselves. That's the way it was. We had nothing. We made the goalie nets ourselves and we used them again in the summer to play soccer. When we were very young we made a smaller rink and later a regular size rink"

Serge's father owned a butter factory and was the town mayor for 40 years. Hockey was very important to the Savard family. On the living room wall there were three pictures: one was of the Quebec premier, one was the pope and one was Rocket Richard, the legendary scoring star of the Montreal Canadiens.

When Serge was a young boy, his dad gave him a simple but important piece of advice: "Be a good person." It became his guiding principle on and off the ice as long as he played the game.

He and his friends played 5-on-5 games on local ponds with Serge pretending he was his hero, Jean Beliveau. "We lived right in front of the church. We had to go every morning and at night at seven o'clock was the rosary on radio and all the lights had to be turned off on the ice. But we skipped the radio broadcast. We turned the lights off but we kept skating."

"Hockey was *the* thing. It was *everything* to us. We'd spend 50 hours a week on the ice. Kids today have the choice of 200 TV channels, the choice of all kinds of sports. We didn't have television until I was nine years old so we didn't see hockey games. We didn't see the Montreal Canadiens, but that's all we talked about. For young Quebecers like me, our dream was playing hockey for the Canadiens. We didn't think for one second about playing for anyone else."

Serge didn't play organized hockey until he was 9. By that time he was growing like a weed. "When I turned 10, my father put me in a boarding school in Montreal with my brother. There were ice rinks everywhere. From age 10-15 I really improved."

At 11 years of age Serge stood six feet tall and towered over his teammates. He could have used his size to bulldoze smaller players, but he preferred to use his speed and skill to get around them. In fact, Serge and his friends didn't hit each other at all, and they didn't fight. He didn't like that part of the game.

By the time he turned 15, he was 6'3" and weighed 200 pounds! "There was a scout who saw me play at school in Rouyn and he referred me to the Montreal Canadiens. They invited me to the Junior Canadiens training camp." He proved to be a quiet leader and was soon named team captain.

Before long Serge, from tiny Landrienne, was playing for the team that every young Quebecer idolized. The team he and his friends had only been able to listen to on the radio. "Back then most Montreal Canadiens players came from small places like mine."

Even though he stood out as the biggest and best player on every team he played for, he always thought of himself as part of a team. That was the most important thing to him. "If you play for a team and you break all the records and the team doesn't win, it's no fun," he said.

After reaching the NHL, Serge ended up winning eight Stanley Cups in 11 years and countless individual awards. The one he's proudest of is the Bill Masterton Memorial Trophy "for the player who best exemplifies the qualities of perseverance, sportsmanship and dedication to hockey." Most people thought that defensemen had to be too rough and tough to win such an award. Savard proved that it could be done. As he accepted the trophy he thought back to his father's advice: be a good person.

~

In Sault Ste Marie, Ontario, brothers **Tony** and **Phil Esposito** played hockey at every opportunity. Tony was usually a goalie and Phil liked to skate and score. Each morning before daybreak, they grabbed flashlights and headed out into the darkness. They put their hockey gear on a toboggan and dragged it to the outdoor rink, where they played until it was time for school. After supper they played outside until they could barely see the puck.

Then they'd hear their father's whistle. That was the signal that it was time to come home. But that didn't mean the hockey was over. It had just moved indoors—to the basement or bedrooms.

Sometimes their ingenious mom even used their love of hockey to get the housework done. She tied cloth diapers on the boys' elbows and knees and invited them to play on their hands and knees. She was the goalie and the puck was their dad's wool sock. They played hockey and shined the floor all at the same time.

Phil and Tony were very close in age so they always had someone to play with and against. Like most brothers and sisters, they were very competitive. One time they wrestled in the basement rec room and slammed against the wall, leaving a humungous hole. They were too afraid to tell their parents so they hung a calendar over the hole and kept playing. It stayed there for years, until their parents noticed it.

Older brother Phil made it to the NHL first, signing with the Boston Bruins. As luck would have it, when Tony arrived with the Montreal Canadiens, his first game was against his brother's team. The game ended in a 2-2 tie with Phil scoring both goals against his brother.

The two teams played each other again two weeks later. This game ended in a 0-0 tie and several of Tony's 41 saves were against his older brother. Fans soon began calling him Tony 0 because he was racking up so many shutouts.

It seemed that wherever the Esposito boys went they ended up together. And now both are together in the Hockey Hall of Fame.

In Timmins, Ontario the **Mahovlich** brothers, **Frank and Peter**, didn't play against each other at all. At least not until they reached the NHL. Frank was almost ten years older than Pete. By the time Pete was eight, Frank was playing junior hockey. And by the time he turned 12, Frank was already a star in the NHL with the Toronto Maple Leafs. But in spite of the age difference they were very close.

Frank and Pete were the sons of immigrants from Croatia. Their father worked in the gold mines near Timmins for 25 years before moving the family to Leaside in Toronto. For many years he sharpened skates for young hockey players in the neighbourhood.

The boys were very different. Frank was quiet and serious and moody. Pete was outgoing and full of fun.

When Peter reached the NHL, it was natural for people to make comparisons between the two brothers. His parents had been careful not to put pressure on their younger son. Frank was 6'0 and weighed 200 pounds when he joined the Toronto Maple Leafs. They called him the "Big M." When Pete arrived in the NHL he was 6'5" and weighed 215. He could have been called the "Bigger M", but no such luck. Instead, he was always known as Frank's "little brother."

~

These Canadian boys grew up at different times and in different places. They faced the usual problems that all kids have. They worried about fitting in, about being popular, about concerns at school and at home. Some had physical problems they had to overcome.

They all had hockey. They had natural talent but that alone wasn't enough. They all worked hard to improve. They all found ways to overcome challenges. If they needed help they found people who could help them. Most important, they never gave up.

Meanwhile, in villages and towns on the other side of the world, Russian boys had also grown up loving hockey. They also had talent and they also worked hard to get better. They had their own worries and challenges. And they had their own hockey dreams.

These two groups of boys, now men, were about to meet face to face on the ice – with the entire world watching.

2: The big idea

By 1972, these young Canadian boys were grown up and playing in the NHL, battling each other night after night in pursuit of hockey's biggest prize, the Stanley Cup. Fierce rivals like the Montreal Canadiens and Toronto Maple Leafs fought with everything they had to reach the playoffs. Their goal was to help their team win, not to become friends with players on other teams. It's not surprising that there were often bad feelings between players throughout the league. They were playing for money and bragging rights and for their fans. They wore their jerseys with great pride. That's just the way it was in pro hockey.

And then—just like that—the best players in the NHL were asked to forget those fierce rivalries. Suddenly they were asked to wear a new jersey, one with a large red Canadian maple leaf on it. They were asked to play for Team Canada against a brand new foe.

It was like a real-life video quest game. They were about to set out on a mission that would take them across Canada and across the ocean into a realm that was very mysterious and full of risks and pitfalls. The reward that waited at the end was worth fighting for, but it would take all their abilities and skills to complete the mission successfully.

They played for Montreal and Toronto and New York and Boston and Buffalo and Detroit and Chicago. Some were already stars, others were full of potential. Each of these players had fans across Canada, but before they were finished they would turn the second largest country on the planet into a single community, all cheering wildly for them.

Meanwhile, in the USSR, a group of players had a quest of their own. They had been brought together to play for the Soviet Union on a team made up of members of the Red Army team. They were the very best players in their country. They wanted to show that they were also the best in the world. And that meant they had to beat the best of the NHL.

In 1972, everyone who knew hockey was convinced that Canada was the greatest hockey country on earth. It was as sure as the sun rising every morning. After all, the National Hockey League was the best hockey league in the world and 95% of NHL players were Canadians.

The players definitely thought they were the best. The sports writers and other experts continuously told Canadians they were best, and Canadian fans believed they were the best.

And then something happened that made them doubt that belief. Something that sent shock waves across the country from Newfoundland to British Columbia.

~

It's true that for many years Canada had lost to the Soviet Union in the Olympics, but that was only because, at that time, professional athletes were not allowed to compete. The Olympics were strictly for amateur athletes.

The Soviet Union gathered together the best 20 "amateur" players from across their country of 150 million to play against other nations.

Meanwhile the best 500 players from Canada—a massive country but with a population of just 20 million—were not allowed to play in international competitions because they were being paid to play in the National Hockey League. Instead, Canada sent university players to represent us at the Olympics.

The problem was that the Russians weren't really amateurs, either.

They were paid big salaries as officers in the soviet Red Army, even though their one and only job was to play hockey. Canadians thought it was unfair.

After much discussion, a group of Canadians came up with a plan to prove once and for all which country had the top hockey players. The NHLers would play the Russians in an eight-game series. The first four games would be played in Canada and the last four in Moscow. It would be our best against their best.

They decided to call it the **Summit Series**.

Most people thought that it would be an easy series for the Canadians. After all, the Russians had inferior skates, inferior sticks, and inferior uniforms. They had strange training systems and new strategies on the ice. They would almost certainly be humiliated. Many predicted an eight game sweep.

A few experts disagreed. They had observed the Russians play and they could see their talent and discipline. But there weren't many who listened to these warnings. Canadians from coast to coast couldn't wait for the series to start.

There was another reason why the Summit Series was getting so much attention. In 1972, democratic countries like Canada and the United States were in the middle of a cold war with the USSR (the Soviet Union). Cold wars aren't fought with guns, tanks and airplanes. They are fought with propaganda, threats, distrust, and fear. The USSR was said to be "behind the Iron Curtain", meaning that it was a closed society.

Both sides were trying to show that they had the best system of government, the best scientists, the best weapons—the best athletes. The United States and the USSR competed to see which country would be first to send a person into space. And which country could send an American astronaut or Soviet cosmonaut to the moon. And when their sports teams met in the Olympics, the athletes played with extra determination.

~

Once the details for the Summit Series were worked out and the contracts were signed, Canadian organizers had to pick 35 NHL players to join Team Canada. Harry Sinden, who had once played for Canada in the Olympics, was hired as the coach.

Sinden and his assistant coach, John Ferguson, met with organizer Alan Eagleson to decide who to invite. Some choices were obvious. They were the very best the NHL had to offer. The stars and superstars. Others needed more thought.

Bobby Orr was considered the best player in the league, but he couldn't play because of a knee injury. Bobby Hull, a great scoring threat, couldn't go because he had just left the NHL to play in a new league called the WHA.

Phil Esposito was a natural choice. He was at the top of his game. He had just won the Stanley Cup with the Boston Bruins (1971-72 season). He scored 66 goals and won the Art Ross Trophy with 130 points. He was named the playoff MVP, leading the Bruins past the New York Rangers. The year before that, he set a new NHL record with 76 goals and had added 76 assists.

Brad Park was also one of the first to be chosen. The great defenseman played for the New York Rangers, who had just lost to the Bruins in the Cup final.

Paul Henderson, Ron Ellis, and Bobby Clarke were surprise selections. They were younger and didn't have as much experience as the others. Serge Savard was chosen for his speed and his size. He had already won two Stanley Cups for Montreal. Phil Esposito was joined by his goaltender brother Tony. Frank and Pete Mahovlich would have a chance to play together at last.

Finally a group of 35 players was decided on and invited to join the Canadian team. At first they were going to call themselves the NHL All-Stars but it was decided that a new name was needed. Someone came up with the name Team Canada and it stuck.

But while they were now officially members of Team Canada, they were far from being a team in the truest sense of the word. In those days, players from other teams didn't like each other very much and often didn't speak to each other, even during the off-seasons. The feeling was that this kind of friendliness would make them too soft and unwilling to deliver a hard body check when needed. The Boston Bruins had just won the 1971-72 Stanley Cup in a tough battle against the NY Rangers and now Bruins and Rangers players were supposed to act like buddies?

As this point they were just a bunch of talented professional players from different teams who had been selected to represent Canada. In fact, they were an all-star team of strangers. They didn't know each other except as ice enemies. During the long NHL season, they had fought tooth and nail against each other. That's what they were paid to do and that's what their fans expected. They were all stars and now they were being asked to make unselfish passes to former foes, and to stand up for each other for the good of the team. It would prove to be their biggest challenge.

3: A shocking start

Game One was played in the famous Montreal Forum on September 2, 1972, a very warm night, inside the rink and out. In the Canadian dressing room before the game, the Canadian players were relaxed and joking with each other. There was little or no respect for their Russian opponents. The Canadian players thought it would be easy.

"We thought they'd be pushovers," Henderson said.

The Prime Minister of Canada, Pierre Trudeau, dropped the ceremonial first puck and the 18,818 Forum fans and a TV audience in the millions across Canada settled in for an entertaining hockey game. They were confident of a win.

Fans had barely settled into their seats when Canadian superstar Phil Esposito scored in the first 30 seconds. Happy fans cheered and smiled at each other knowingly. When Paul Henderson followed with a goal at the 6:32 mark, the smiles turned into grins and slaps on the back. This was going to be easy.

The Soviets seemed disorganized and sloppy, overwhelmed by the idea of playing against national heroes in front of the largest crowd they'd ever seen.

And then, as if someone had flicked a switch, everything changed. Suddenly the Soviets were like a different team. Their passes were crisp and accurate. They showed poise and patience. They played unselfishly, pass after pass until they had a scoring chance.

Less than 10 minutes into the game, with the Canadians still leading by two goals, the Clarke, Ellis, Henderson line came off the ice winded after a shift in which they were chasing the Soviets all around the ice. The players couldn't believe what was happening.

"Paul and I are sitting there huffing and puffing," says Ellis. "Paul looked at me and said, 'Ron, this is going to be a long series.' We knew at the two minute mark. We were huffing and puffing and my chest was burning and the Russians were dancing."

Sure enough, the Russians beat goalie Ken Dryden twice to tie the score before the end of the first period. The NHLers were shocked. The Russians were skating circles around them. They were full of energy while the professionals already looked tired.

The second period was no better. Russian speedster Valerie Kharlamov scored twice within ten minutes. The Canadian defence was no match for the skilful moves of the 5'8", 165 lb forward. He skated past them as if they were standing still.

"They were two beautiful goals," says Ellis

Clarke scored for Canada to open the third period, but it was too little and too late. The Soviets went on to score three more times to seal a 7-3 win.

The Montreal Forum crowd was stunned into silence. Fans at home had expected a celebration. It was as if you had invited someone to your birthday party and they let the air out of all the balloons. The whole country felt deflated.

The dressing room after the game was as quiet as a library. No one spoke or even looked at their teammates. Heads hung low, partly from exhaustion and partly from embarrassment. Players had given it their best individual efforts but it wasn't nearly enough to match the team effort of these unknowns from behind the Iron Curtain.

The Russians had taken the Canadian game and added their own twists. "They had invented a new way of playing hockey," observed CBC-TV producer Ralph Mellanby. It was up to Canada to find an answer.

The Russian dressing room was also quiet but it was the quiet confidence that comes after a job well done. They had performed efficiently like cogs in a well-oiled machine, every person doing his job to support the others.

Newspapers the next day were full of doom and gloom. WE LOST, screamed one Montreal newspaper headline

Some called it a wakeup call. Coach Sinden disagreed. "I was awake all the time. The rest of them were sleeping. Our players were overconfident. Cocky. The Russians were on the same level as the NHL players."

Serge Savard was one of the few members of Team Canada who was not surprised. Savard had played against Soviet teams once before when he was a member of the Junior Canadiens.

"I knew what good athletes they were," he said. "But during the weeks of training camp you read in the paper every day how good we were. They said they would not win one game. We had people scouting them who said they couldn't shoot the puck. We all became as a group overconfident. We came back to earth very quickly in the first game. There is no doubt that they were in better shape. They trained 11 months a year in those days."

"They had fantastic conditioning," adds coach Sinden.

The entire country was in shock. It was as if the world no longer made sense. How could this be happening?

In Moscow and all across the Soviet Union, there was joy and celebration. Even though Soviet teams had won the last three Olympics and nine of the most recent international tournaments, this was different. They had tested themselves against the NHL, the best of the best. And they had passed the test with flying colours.

The next game was three days later, a Monday, in Toronto's Maple Leaf Gardens. For players and fans, the wait seemed to go on forever.

The Canadians looked closely at what had happened in Game One and made some changes. Serge Savard was added to the lineup and Tony O replaced Ken Dryden in net. Savard always played well under pressure and was a calming influence on defence.

Esposito opened the scoring for Canada at 7:14 of the second period. Early in the third, Yvan Cournoyer showed everyone why he had earned the nickname Roadrunner. He outskated the Russian defenders and put the puck past Vladislav Tretiak in the Russian net.

Soviet star Alexander Yakushev scored four minutes later on a power play to cut the Canadian lead to a single goal and the Maple Leaf Garden fans held their collective breath, fearing another collapse. To make things even worse, Canada was then assessed a penalty. But it was at this point that Pete Mahovlich took control. With his mother watching from the stands, Frank's kid brother scored one of the prettiest goals of the series.

Trying to kill the penalty, Phil Esposito cleared the puck from the Canadian zone onto Pete's stick. He entered the Russian zone and faked a slap shot which froze the Russian defenceman. He deked the defender and drove to the net where goalie Tretiak was crouched and waiting. Mahovlich faked a forehand shot, moved to the backhand and snuck the puck past the Soviet goalie. It was a spectacular effort that brought fans to their feet. The Canadian bench emptied as players rushed to congratulate their teammate.

Canada went on to win the game 4-1 to even the series.

Despite the exciting win, Team Canada still wasn't a close-knit unit, although Pete's dramatic goal was a step in that direction. After the game, players still went their separate ways and hung out with friends from their own NHL teams.

With the series tied at one game each, the teams moved to Winnipeg for game three. Tony Esposito was again in nets against Russian goalie Tretiak. Canada jumped out to a 3-1 lead and things were looking good. But the dynamic Kharlamov was relentless, using his speed and lightning-quick moves to make it a one goal contest. The Henderson-Clarke-Ellis line answered less than a minute later, when Henderson put on a burst of speed, caught up with a pass from Clarke, and beat Tretiak on his stick side.

Refusing to give up, the Soviets fought back. Late in the period they put a line of young players on the ice who skated circles around the weary Canadians. The Soviets scored twice to tie the game and that's the way the period and the game, ended, 4-4. A game that had started with so much promise ended with the Canadians desperately hanging on to preserve the tie.

The series was knotted at one win, one loss and one tie each. Only the great play of the man they called Tony O prevented another loss.

The last game played on Canadian soil was in Vancouver. It turned out to be a turning point for Canada for all the wrong reasons. The Soviets scored two power play goals in the first period to take a 2-0 lead.

Fans didn't like the chippy play of the Canadians or the needless penalties that resulted. Boos could be heard in the crowd—not aimed at the Soviets but at the Canadians.

In the second period Canada scored an unassisted goal to make it 2-1, but the Russians answered with two more of their own against Dryden. The capacity crowd of 15,570 were growing restless. The booing got louder, raining down on Team Canada players.

Canada attempted a comeback in the third and scored twice, but the Soviets also scored again. The final score was 5-3. It was the low point of the series.

The Canadian players left the ice with a chorus of boos and jeers echoing in their ears. Only one player remained on the ice.

Phil Esposito, who was named Canadian player of the game, remained for a TV interview at centre ice. With a mixture of sweat and tears on his face, he said, "To the people of Canada, we tried. We gave it our best." He told them how down and how disappointed his teammates were with the fans. "Every one of us came because we love our country. Not for any other reason. We came because we love Canada...Canada is our home. I don't think it's fair that we get booed. We're doing our best. They are a good hockey team. I don't think it's fair that we should be booed."

They were words straight from the heart and Canadians from coast to coast heard them loud and clear. The Canadian players were giving it their best. If they were to turn things around they would need the support of all Canadians. They were headed behind the Iron Curtain. And they had no idea what awaited them there. One thing was certain, they were playing for Canada and win or lose they would never give up.

On the long flight across the Atlantic, players sang *O Canada* over and over again.

Jim Prime

4: Goodbye, Canada. Hello, Russia

When the Canadian players arrived in Moscow, they soon discovered that behind the Iron Curtain everything was very different. There were soldiers with guns on the streets. The language was different. The food was different. The hockey arenas were different.

The Canadians had heard so many stories about spies and secret agents that their imaginations ran wild. There was suspicion and mistrust and fear. They were convinced that they were being followed when they left their hotel. They thought they were being watched all the time. Even in their hotel rooms. They were afraid to talk because they thought the rooms had been bugged with tiny hidden microphones. They thought the

Soviets could hear everything they were saying. Some of their suspicions were justified. Some were not.

Before the series resumed on Soviet soil, a few Canadian players were relaxing in their Moscow hotel room. The more they talked, the more certain they became that they were being spied on. They decided to find the listening devices that they were sure were hidden in the room. They searched and searched. They removed the mattress from the bed and cushions from the sofas. They looked in lamp shades and ceiling lights. They unscrewed light bulbs and examined them closely. They looked under chairs and beds. They looked in the closet and behind pictures on the wall. They removed drawers from the dresser and checked for false bottoms. They even checked behind bathroom mirrors. They looked and looked and found nothing.

And then one player noticed a small lump under the carpet. Very slowly they rolled back the rug and discovered a metal box screwed to the floor.

They were sure they had found the bug. They unscrewed the box. Underneath was another box with more screws. They carefully unscrewed this box too.

Suddenly there was a large crash. They looked through the hole in the floor and saw that a large glass chandelier had hit the floor of the lobby and exploded into a million pieces! Luckily no one was in the lobby at the time.

Some of their suspicions were valid. Phones really were tapped. They got phone calls in their hotel rooms in the middle of the night. When they picked up, no one was there, but their sleep was ruined. Food they had sent over from Canada disappeared. They could only walk in certain places in the city. And couldn't leave the city unless a government agent went with them. Soldiers with machine guns patrolled the streets.

With Canadian's nerves on edge, the first game on Soviet soil finally got underway. The organizers had expected a few hundred Canadians to make the trip to Russia to support the team. There were more than 3000 in the stands that night. They made so much noise it sounded like ten times that many.

The Soviet leader, Leonid Brezhnev, and other important government people were there. The PA announcer introduced the Canadian players, starting with the team captain. "Number 7, Phil Esposito," he said.

Esposito skated toward centre ice and began to wave to the crowd. Suddenly his skates went out from under him and he landed with a loud thump on his behind. The crowd smiled. His teammates smiled. Even Espo smiled. Then he struggled to his feet and took a big bow which made everyone laugh. He blew them a kiss and they laughed harder. It was a nice moment in the middle of a tense showdown.

The Canadian fans continued shouting and singing throughout the game. The Russian fans weren't used to this kind of behaviour. They sat quietly and stiffly in their seats.

One of the Canadian chants was in Russian: "Nyet, nyet Soviet, da da Canada." The crowd was like a seventh player for Canada.

Team Canada was finally united. They had made a stop on the way to Moscow to play some exhibitions against the Swedes. They were beginning to feel comfortable with their linemates. Some players left the team because they weren't getting enough ice time. This made it a tighter, more disciplined group. Egos were being set aside and unselfish play increased.

The team hit the Moscow ice with new confidence. Canada led 1-0 after the first period. In the second frame, Bobby Clarke scored early on a pass from Henderson and just past the halfway mark Clarke returned the favour, as Henderson made it 3-0!

Russia fought back in the third and scored at the 3:34 mark against Tony Esposito who had been brilliant in net for Canada. A minute later Henderson once again answered the call scoring on a pass from Clarke to restore the three goal advantage.

And then disaster struck. The Soviets scored two goals within eight seconds and another two minutes later to tie the game 4-4. The Canadians were in shock, suddenly disorganized and desperate to hang on. Once again they had become overconfident and sloppy. Vlad Vikolov stole the puck in Canada's zone and rushed toward the net, slipping the winning goal past Tony 0 at the 14:46 mark.

Even after the loss, as the players left the ice, the 3000 fans gave them a standing ovation. They knew how hard their team was working. Canada lost that game, but most people who watched it agreed that they had outplayed Russia.

The players knew it, too. In the dressing room after the game they were very down. They had lost a game they should have won. The Russians had now won three games, the Canadians one and there was one tie. Now it was the Soviets who were cocky—after all, they only needed to win one more game to claim the tournament and there were three games left to play. Canada had to win all three to win the series. It seemed impossible.

Phil Esposito and Paul Henderson did their best to lift their spirits. "We're not going to lose another game," promised Espo.

The next morning was like Christmas, as thousands and thousands of telegrams arrived. "They hit us in waves," said Phil Esposito. Green garbage bags were filled to the brim with letters and telegrams.

The players got together and sorted through them. They were from every province and territory, all of them wishing Team Canada well. The bags stretched all the way down the corridor to their dressing room. It was like all of Canada was with them in the arena.

Game 6 was two days later, on September 24. It remained to be seen if the Canadians had learned from their mistakes. Would they be able to shake off the gut-wrenching loss and use it to inspire them? Or would they fold to the relentless Soviets who were now heavy favourites to win the series?

With the odds stacked against them they approached Game 6 with steely determination. Losing was not an option.

The two teams battled through a scoreless first period, with Canada forced to kill off two penalties. People would talk about the second period for years to come.

The Soviets scored at the 1:12 mark to give them a 1-0 lead, but Bobby Hull's younger brother Dennis tied it minutes later. The Roadrunner, Yvan Cournoyer, gave Canada the lead at 6:21, and fifteen seconds later the lad from Lucknow, Paul Henderson, intercepted a pass at centre ice, streaked across the Russian blue line, and beat Tretiak on a low drive that sneaked past the post and settled into the netting. Yakushev scored a late power-play goal to bring the period to a close with Canada clinging to a 3-2 lead.

The Soviets laid siege to the Canadian net in the third, unleashing 17 shots at Ken Dryden, but the Montreal Canadiens goalie withstood the barrage and Canada emerged with the win.

An ugly incident marred what should have been a glorious victory. Valeri Kharlamov, a compact ball of energy and talent had been a constant threat to the Canadians throughout the series. The left winger's speed and puck-handling skills made him MVP in Game One and earned him the respect of Canadian hockey fans. After that game Ronnie Ellis had been assigned to cover him and had done a masterful job, holding him to 3 goals and 4 assists.

With Canada leading 3-2 halfway through the second period of Game 6, Bobby Clarke decided to slow the Russian star down. In the NHL, Clarke had the reputation for being very aggressive, very physical, playing just within the rules—and sometimes outside the rules. He chased Kharlamov down and delivered a two-handed chop with his stick, breaking his ankle.

The players on the Team Canada bench had been told to stop Kharlamov and Clarke admits that he set out to do just that. "I don't brag about it. I don't talk about it. I just did it. [But] I didn't try to break his ankle."

Physical intimidation was always part of Clarke's game. Ron Ellis remembers that, when the Summit Series was over and his Toronto Maple Leafs played Clarke's Philadelphia Flyers in NHL action, nothing had changed. The very first time the two Team Canada line mates faced off, "Clarke speared me," he says. "We had just become very close—but that's Bobby Clarke."

Serge Savard wasn't surprised, either. "[Clarke] did the same thing to Kharlamov that he would do to me. He got me in the ankle a few times. [I wore] ankle guards because that's the way he was doing things. I like Bobby—I became friends with Bobby Clarke—but that doesn't mean I agreed with what he was doing."

Paul Henderson looks back at the play with sadness. "I hated their [government] systems. I hated that they pretended to be amateurs. Unfortunately, we took it out on the players. They turned out to be really, really nice people."

Years later Savard, the defenceman who hated violence, helped to vote Kharlamov into the Hockey Hall of Fame. "I presented him and he got in. I thought he was their best player."

After another off day to lick their wounds, the two teams faced off in the seventh game of the eight-game series. The Canadians again came out flying. It was another tight game with Tony Esposito back in net. His brother Phil scored first, with assists from Ronnie Ellis and Paul Henderson, but Yakushev tied it on sizzling slapshot that froze Tony 0.

The Soviets took the lead on a power-play goal by Vladimir Petrov. But there was no quit in Team Canada. Savard performed one of his famous spinarama moves to avoid a Soviet defender and laid the puck on Phil

Esposito's stick. The Russians seemed unable to stop the big man when he was anywhere near the net. The tireless centre propelled a quick, hard shot past Tretiak to knot the score 2-2 after the first period.

Following a scoreless second, Canada took control early in the third as they scored on a goal by Rod Gilbert. But referees took the wind from their sails, calling a holding penalty on defenseman Gary Bergman.

The Soviets quickly took advantage on the power play. Their top scorer, Yakushev, another master around the net, scored on a tip-in. Once again the score was tied.

As the minutes and seconds ticked by, it looked like the game would end in a tie, which would have ended any chance of Canada winning the series.

With less than four minutes to go in regulation time, the referee called roughing majors against both teams, meaning that they would be playing four-on-four hockey for the rest of the game.

With three minutes left, Sinden sent out the Henderson-Clarke–Ellis line. With the play deep in Canadian territory, Serge Savard fought to get the puck to Henderson, who streaked down the right wing across centre ice and cut toward the left wing. He made a slick move to get past one Soviet backchecker and bore down on two burly defensemen who stood between him and the goal. Somehow he managed to get past the first man with the puck on his stick, manoeuvred past the second defender who tripped him, and bore down on Tretiak.

As he was falling, he saw an opening above the goalie's shoulder and lifted the puck just under the crossbar for the winning goal.

It was one of the prettiest goals of the series and a spectacular individual effort. His teammates mobbed him. It was Henderson's second game-winning tally in two games, and the Canadian fans went wild. Back home, celebrations erupted in every city, town and village. Canada had won 4-3!

The series was tied at 3 wins each with one tie. The final game would be for all the marbles. All across Canada fans were on the edge of their seats, longing for a storybook finish—one with a happy ending.

5: The goal

It was Thursday, September 28, 1972. The Luzhniki Ice Palace in Moscow was packed to the rafters with nervous and excited fans. There was less than a minute to go in the final game of the biggest hockey series in Canadian and Russian history. The score stood at 5-5. The best movie-makers in the world could not have devised a more exciting script. The two teams had fought tooth and nail for almost a full month and there was still no winner.

The series was deadlocked. The quest to be best was nearing its climactic finish.

Back home in Canada, TVs had been wheeled into school classrooms so that students could watch history being made. Office buildings were half-empty as workers called in sick so they could watch at home. Farmers did their chores early so they could follow the game. Fishermen listened on short wave radios.

There was almost no traffic on city streets and highways. The whole country seemed frozen in time, all because of a hockey game.

The game began badly for Team Canada. They drew two penalties in the first five minutes and the Soviets took advantage with a power play goal by Yakushev, who had been matching Esposito goal for goal throughout the eight games.

A Russian player was called for interference and Esposito responded with a power play goal for Canada.

But the penalties for Canada kept coming, and when Cournoyer was called for interference, the Russians once again took a one-goal lead on a goal set up by the valiant Kharlamov, who was attempting to play despite his serious ankle injury. Again Canada countered, this time on a goal by Brad Park.

The first period ended with the score tied 2-2. The players on both teams were giving it their all. They left the ice drained of every ounce of energy. Emotions were running high in the stands as well as on the ice. Canadian players thought that many of the penalty calls were unfair, and the Canadian fans agreed.

In the second period, Team Canada found themselves in a deep hole. The Soviets scored three times, the first at the 21 second mark. Amazingly, all three were unassisted goals, one by Yakushev, who seemed unstoppable. Canada managed only a lone goal.

The score was now 5-3 for the Soviets. Canadian chances were fading fast.

The Canadians stormed out of the dressing room for the third period determined to play the best twenty minutes of hockey they could muster. Somehow they had dug deep within themselves and discovered a new reserve of energy somewhere.

Leading the charge was—who else—Phil Esposito, who was playing like an oversized Energizer Bunny with batteries that never ran down. He already had six goals and four assists in the series, to lead all Canadian scorers. Before the period was over he would have seven goals and two more assists.

The Canadians had talked it over in the dressing room between periods. They knew they had to score early in the third period to have a chance to come back.

Pete Mahovlich fought for the puck along the boards and lobbed it in Phil Esposito's direction. He knocked the pass out of the air and put it past Tretiak at the 2:27 mark to narrow Russia's lead to one goal, 5-4. Canada was on a roll.

Ten minutes later, Esposito stormed down the ice, battling his way past a trio of Russian defenders, and sent a shot toward the net that rebounded to Yvan Cournoyer. Cournoyer backhanded the puck past a diving Tretiak to tie the game with just under seven minutes left to play.

The Canadians had been given extra incentive between periods. The Soviets made it crystal clear that if the game ended in a tie they would declare victory because they had scored more goals over the course of the series. Team Canada had seven minutes to shut down the high-powered Soviet scoring machine and notch a goal.

They had started out as a group of individual NHL stars but they had learned that individual talent wasn't enough. It had taken a while to figure that out but they were now a team.

In reality, it had started many years before that, back when they were young boys skating on backyard rinks and neighbourhood ponds. That was where the raw talent developed into true skill. That was where the idea of teamwork was learned. They had faced a variety of challenges to make it to the top of their profession. They all had faced disappointment. They had fought to overcome personal challenges. They all had their own stories to tell.

They were no longer cocky. They knew that the Russians were a great team and they respected them. But they did have a confidence that had been missing for awhile.

They also knew that back home their friends and neighbours were pulling for them every time they were on the ice. Their fellow Canadians —people they had never met—were counting on them. They could feel it from thousands of kilometres away. They could hear it in the arena where 3000 fans sounded more like 30,000.

And then everything seemed to slow down, as if they were in a dream.

Strange things began to happen. Magical things. Miraculous things.

The line of Pete Mahovlich, Esposito and Cournoyer were on the ice. With a minute remaining, Henderson stood up and shouted at Pete to come off the ice. Peter thought it was the coach speaking and skated to the bench. It was an unusual move, even bizarre, but Paul just had a feeling he could score.

He sprung over the boards and took Pete's place.

Yvan, the Roadrunner, had the puck on the opposite side of the ice as Paul sped into position. Yvan's pass was off the mark and Henderson shot awkwardly, missed and was tripped by the Soviet defenseman. He slid into the boards behind Tretiak. While he struggled to get up, Esposito desperately shot the puck at the net.

Tretiak made the save, but the puck was still alive. Henderson tried to bury the rebound, but again the Russian goalie stopped it.

Miraculously, the puck again rebounded onto Henderson's stick and this time he made no mistake. The puck was behind Tretiak at the back of the net. Canada was ahead 6-5 with 34 seconds on the clock.

Henderson admitted later that it was the most beautiful ugly goal he ever scored.

"When I watched the winning goal go over the goal line into the net, I thought of my dad," Henderson said years later. "I hadn't thought of him through the whole series, but I thought of him then. I thought back to when he let me know how proud he was of me. I said out loud, *Dad would have loved this one.* I had a brief moment of sadness that he wasn't there to see it and then I jumped into Cournoyer's arms to celebrate."

Ellis recalls, "There was so much going on when he scored. The emotions, fighting back to tie the game. The Russians sending someone around to tell us that if the game remained tied they were going to declare victory because they had more goals in the series. That happened just after we tied it 5-all. What a great motivator for us. It just spurred us on and when Paul scored that goal I was one of the first over the boards. We were all huddled together. We started chanting, 'We did it! We did it!'"

The members of Team Canada were little boys again, skating on the backyard rinks in Flin Flon and Landrienne and Sault Ste Marie, pretending they were Gordie Howe or Jean Beliveau—pretending to score the biggest goal of their lives. Except that this was real. This dream had come true.

In fact even their childhood dreams had never been this big. Their names were now household words back home: Espo, Tony O, Hendy, Ronnie, Bobby, Serge and all the rest. They were no longer an NHL all-star team. They were no longer representing the Maple Leafs or Canadiens or Flyers. They would always be members of Team Canada '72, the team that came together to beat the Soviets.

"Little did I know back then that I would be involved in one of the most famous hockey series in Canadian history let alone score three winning goals," Henderson says. "All these years later, people still want to shake my hand and let me know what an important moment it was in their lives."

He adds, "When people praise me for scoring the goals, including the Game 8 winner, I know it's not me that they want to honour. It's hockey. It's Canada. When we win on the ice every Canadian feels they won."

Canada is a huge country. Each province and region is unique. Each has its own concerns. The provinces don't always agree and sometimes that causes bad feelings. The Summit Series showed that these differences are just family squabbles. At the end of the day, we're still family and we can work together for the good of everyone in it.

The Summit Series reminded us that no matter where we come from, we are all Canadians. When Paul Henderson scored his goal, no one on the ice was thinking about their differences. They were thinking about all the happy people back home in Canada. There was only pride in coming together to defeat a worthy opponent.

Henderson still marvels at how this group of players from across Canada put aside regional differences for the good of the team. "When Toronto is playing Montreal it's more than just a game," he says. "It's as if it's one country is battling another. But with Team Canada there was none of that. Suddenly we were all Canadians. We were Team Canada and all of Canada was united behind us."

There was pride, national pride and pride that they refused to give up. They played with heart. They won with heart. They learned and adapted.

"It was as close to war as I'll ever experience," says Ron Ellis. "It was one way of life against another. Canada believed that we were the birthplace of the game and they were trying to take something that was ours away from us."

He adds, "Don't ever count out the Canadians."

6: Looking back/looking ahead

The world has changed a lot since 1972. The Soviet Union no longer exists. In 1991, the 19 republics declared themselves independent states. Russia, the largest country with 148 million people, continues to be a world power and a hockey power.

Hockey has changed a lot since 1972, too. The NHL has doubled from 16 to 32 teams and includes players from all over the world—sixteen countries in all. Canada still has more than half of the league's professional players, but the United States and Sweden have hundreds of players spread throughout the league. Russia, once our bitter enemy on the ice, now has 55 players playing alongside Canadians on various teams.

Canadian fans collect the hockey cards of Russian players. Some Russians, like Alex Ovechkin, have become heroes to many Canadian fans. Talent is now the only criterion for playing in the NHL.

The growth of girl's hockey is skyrocketing.

In 1972 many people thought hockey was just a boy's game. They thought it was too rough for girls. They were dead wrong. Women now play the game at the highest levels.

In 1998, women's hockey became an Olympic sport, and since then Canadian women have captured five Olympic gold medals.

One of their biggest supporters is Bobby Clarke. "I think women's hockey is ahead of the men in some ways," he says. "Let's face it, we like contact and we like body checking but in women's hockey they play a game that the NHL could learn from. When they go to check somebody they are going to get the puck. That's what the men should be doing."

Paul Henderson agrees. "The skill level of these girls is incredible and it's fun to watch," he says. "Our national women's team can fire the puck and skate and pass."

The Hockey Hall of Fame has changed as well. Eight women have now been inducted into the institution that honours the greatest players in the history of the game. "This is not the Men's Hall of Fame, it's the Hockey Hall of Fame," says Ken Dryden. "Of course women should be in it."

Soviet stars of the Summit Series, Valeri Kharlamov, Alexander Yakushev, and Vladislov Tretiak, have been added to the great players who are honoured there. Team Canada '72 is now enshrined as a group, and fifteen members of that team are also in the HHOF as individuals, including Serge Savard, Bobby Clarke, Frank Mahovlich and brother Pete, and Phil Esposito and his brother Tony.

The line of Paul Henderson, Ron Ellis and Bobby Clarke was the most effective during the series. They look back to '72 with pride.

"It was the highlight of my hockey career," Ron Ellis says. "I was at my peak as a player. Paul and Clarkie and I played all eight games together. It was a miracle finish. We won the last three games by one goal each. We made Canada very proud and brought the country together. We were able to work through adversity. We adapted to their style and we didn't quit. We kept fighting and kept together. We gave it our best. I think the game is better off today because of that series."

He adds, "I think the Russians have adapted some of our style. They play a little more aggressively now. These guys were tough, it just wasn't part of their game. I wouldn't want to meet some of the guys we played against in a dark alley. The game is better because now it's a combination of both styles."

Summing up, Ellis says, "I felt that both teams won. We won a very slim victory with 34 seconds to go in Game Eight. The Russians proved to the world that they could play with the best—with Canada's best. With a break or two they could have beaten us. That's why I think both teams won. The Summit Series taught me that you should never give up on the Canadians. We won't win every game but we are coming to play every time we skate on the ice. Our ancestors never gave up on Canada. They built this country in the face of great difficulties."

Pete Mahovlich agrees. "We won but they didn't lose," he says.

Serge Savard thinks that it was the players' love of Canada that allowed them to come back from a terrible start and win the series. "I don't think an athlete could have elevated himself as high as we did in '72 if not for that. It meant a lot more to us because we were representing our country. It was more than that because we got caught in the middle of a war. There were two systems that were comparing themselves. I think the Russians were trying to show the world that the Communist system was the best system in the world. And they were trying to show the world by showing off their athletes, like they always did at the Olympics. We were caught in the middle of that. We had to prove it's not true."

Savard won eight Stanley Cups with the Montreal Canadiens but he calls the Summit Series "the biggest thrill of my sports career. I put it ahead of any Stanley Cups I won. It meant a lot more to us because we represented our country."

Even in this hard-fought, emotional series he continued to heed the words of his father: *Be a good person.* "I didn't hate the Soviet players. I really admired their skill. I did not have one penalty in the whole Summit Series, not one. We won four and tied one in the five games I was in. So it's not the tough guys that won the series, it was the skilled players who won the series."

Paul Henderson often thinks back to the days in Lucknow when he got his first pair of skates. "Little did I know back then that I would be involved in the most famous hockey series in Canadian history, let alone score three winning goals. My goal in the final game had a huge impact on me and on the country I love. It changed my own life. I know that I don't deserve as much credit as I got. And I know that fame alone can't make you happy."

Henderson adds, "Canada is so huge that sometimes it seems like we are very divided. But with Team Canada '72 there was none of that. Suddenly we were all Canadians. All our differences were cast aside. We were Team Canada and all of Canada was united behind us. Not everyone is a hockey fan and that's okay. But when Canada plays, everyone becomes a fan. When we win on the ice most Canadians feel they've won."

Bobby Clarke, the tough kid from Flin Flon, remembers how Russian kids used to follow Team Canada players as they walked down the street in Moscow. "There were always kids around us and we kept things in our pockets for them. We had bags of gum and candy and other stuff to give them. It was really neat."

Years after the Summit Series was over Clarke sat down with Russian players to talk about hockey. "In 1986 I had Tretiak out to my house. Over the years I found that as soon as you got away from the game, the Russians were no different from us really. They were just hockey players. They couldn't have cared less about politics."

Why did the series mean so much to us? There are many reasons.

As Canadians we learned a lot about ourselves. We learned what we can do when we work together. We learned that we have many more similarities than differences. We learned that if you want something enough and are willing to work to overcome obstacles, you can accomplish amazing things.

We also learned that hockey is bigger than any one country. We learned that boys and girls all over the world love the game too. And their dreams aren't all that different from our own.

The teams

G = goalie D = defenseman   RW = right wing LW= left wing C = centre

Team Canada

1 Ed Johnston – G, Boston Bruins
2 Gary Bergman - D, Detroit Red Wings
3 Pat Stapleton - D, Chicago Blackhawks
4 Bobby Orr - D, Boston Bruins
5 Brad Park – D, NY Rangers
6 Ron Ellis – RW, Toronto Maple Leafs
7 Phil Esposito – C, Boston Bruins
8 Rod Gilbert – RW, NY Rangers
9 Bill Goldsworthy – RW, Minnesota North Stars
10 Dennis Hull – LW, Chicago Blackhawks
11 Vic Hadfield – LW, NY Rangers
12 Yvan Cournoyer – RW Montreal Canadiens
14 Wayne Cashman – RW, Boston Bruins
15 Red Berenson – C, Detroit Red Wings
16 Rod Seiling – D, NY Rangers
17 Bill White – D, Chicago Blackhawks
18 Jean Ratelle – C, NY Rangers
19 Paul Henderson – LW, Toronto Maple Leafs

20 Pete Mahovlich – LW, Montreal Canadiens
21 Stan Mikita – C, Chicago Blackhawks
22 J. P. Parise – LW, Minnesota North Stars
23 Serge Savard – D, Montreal Canadiens
24 Mickey Redmond – RW, Detroit Red Wings
25 Guy Lapointe – D, Montreal Canadiens
26 Don Awrey – D, Boston Bruins
27 Frank Mahovlich – LW, Montreal Canadiens
28 Bobby Clarke – LW, Philadelphia Flyers
29 Ken Dryden – G, Montreal Canadiens
32 Dale Tallon – D, Vancouver Canucks
33 Gilbert Pereault – C, Buffalo Sabres
34 Marcel Dionne – C, Detroit Red Wings
35 Tony Esposito – G, Chicago Blackhawks
36 Richard Martin – LW, Buffalo Sabres
37 Jocelyn Guevremont – D, Vancouver Canucks
38 Brian Glennie – D, Toronto Maple Leafs

Coaches

Harry Sinden, Head Coach/GM
John Ferguson, Assistant Coach

G = goalie D = defenseman   RW = right wing LW= left wing C = centre

Team USSR

1 Victor Zinger – G, Spartak M
2 Alexander Gusev – D, CSKA
3 Vladimir Lutchenko – D, CSKA
4 Viktor Kuzkin – D, CSKA
5 Alexander Ragulin – D, CSKA
6 Valery Vasiliev – D, Dynamo M
7 Gennady Tsygankov – D, CSKA
8 Vyacheslav Starshinov – C, Spartak M
9 Yuri Blinov – LW, CSKA
10 Alexander Maltsev – RW, Dynamo M
11 Yevgeny Zimin – RW, Spartak M
12 Yevgeny Mishakov – LW, CSKA
13 Boris Mikhailov – RW, CSKA
14 Yuri Shatalov – D, Krylya Sovetov
15 Alexander Yakushev – LW, Spartak M
16 Vladimir Petrov – C, CSKA
17 Valery Kharlamov – LW, CSKA

18 Vladimir Vikulov – RW, CSKA
19 Vladimir Shadrin – C, Spartak M
20 Vladislav Tretiak – G, CSKA
21 Vyacheslav Solodukhin – C, SKA L
22 Vyacheslav Anisin – C, Krylya Sovetov
23 Yuri Lebedev – LW, Krylya Sovetov
24 Alexander Bodunov – RW, Krylya Sovetov
25 Yuri Liapkin – D, Khimik
26 Yevgeny Poladiev – D, Spartak M
27 Alexander Sidelnikov – G, Krylya Sovetov
29 Alexander Martynyuk – RW, Spartak M
30 Alexander Volchkov – C, CSKA

Coaches

Vsevolod Bobrov, Head Coach
Boris Kulagin, Assistant Coach

Jim Prime

Top statistics

Soviet players in *italics*.

Goals

Paul Henderson	7
Alexander Yakushev	7
Phil Esposito	7
Valery Kharlamov	3
Vladimir Shadrin	3
Vladimir Petrov	3
Yvan Cournoyer	3
Six tied with 2	

Assists

Phil Esposito	6
Yuri Liapkin	5
Vladimir Shadrin	5
Alexander Maltsev	5
Alexander Yakushev	4
Vladimir Petrov	4
Brad Park	4
Valery Kharlamov	4
Bobby Clarke	4
Six tied with 3	

Penalty minutes

J. P. Parise	28
Bobby Clarke	18
Valery Kharlamov	16
Phil Esposito	15
Wayne Cashman	14
Gary Bergman	13
Vladimir Petrov	10
Boris Mikhailov	9
Rod Gilbert	9
Three tied with 8	

Paul Henderson:
Most Valuable Player of the series

Game summaries

Game 1
MONTREAL   **September 2, 1972**

USSR 7   Canada 3

PLAYERS ON ICE:
Canada: Bergman, Park, Ellis, P. Esposito, Gilbert, Hadfield, Cournoyer, Berenson, Seiling, Ratelle, Henderson, P. Mahovlich, Redmond, Lapointe, Awrey, F. Mahovlich, Clarke

USSR: Gusev, Lutchenko, Kuzkin, Ragulin, Vasiliev, Tsygankov, Blinov, Maltsev, Zimin, Mishakov, Mikhailov, Yakushev, Petrov, Kharlamov, Vikulov, Shadrin, Liapkin, Paladiev

GOALIES:
Canada: Dryden
USSR: Tretiak

FIRST PERIOD
1. Canada - P. Esposito (F. Mahovlich, Bergman) 0:30.
2. Canada - Henderson (Clarke) 6:32.
3. USSR - Zimin (Yakushev, Shadrin) 11:40.
4. USSR - Petrov (Mikhailov) (SHG) 17:28.

Penalties:
Henderson (tripping), 1:03; Yakushev (tripping), 7:04: Mikhailov (tripping), 15:11; Ragulin (tripping), 17:19.

SECOND PERIOD

5. USSR - Kharlamov (Maltsev) 2:40.
6. USSR - Kharlamov (Maltsev) (GWG) 10:18.

Penalties:
Clarke (slashing), 5:16; Lapointe (slashing), 12:53.

THIRD PERIOD

7. Canada - Clarke (Ellis, Henderson) 8:32.
8. USSR - Mikhailov (Blinov) 13:32.
9. USSR - Zimin, 14:29.
10.USSR - Yakushev (Shadrin) 18:37.

Penalties:
Kharlamov (highsticking), 14:45; Lapointe (crosschecking), 19:41.

Shots on goal				
	1	2	3	Total
USSR	10	10	10	30
Canada	10	10	12	32
Game MVPs				
USSR	Kharlamov			
Canada	Clarke			

Game 2
TORONTO   **September 4, 1972**

USSR 1   Canada 4

PLAYERS ON ICE:
Canada: Bergman, Stapleton, Park, Ellis, P. Esposito, Goldsworthy, Cournoyer, Cashman, White, Henderson, P. Mahovlich, Mikita, Parise, Savard, Lapointe, F. Mahovlich, Clarke

USSR: Gusev, Lutchenko, Kuzkin, Ragulin, Tsygankov, Starshinov, Maltsev, Zimin, Mishakov, Mikhailov, Yakushev, Petrov, Kharlamov, Shadrin, Anisin, Liapkin, Paladiev

GOALIES:
Canada: T. Esposito
USSR: Tretiak

FIRST PERIOD
No Scoring.

Penalties:
Park (crosschecking), 10:08; Henderson (tripping), 15:19.

SECOND PERIOD
1. Canada - P. Esposito (Park, Cashman) 7:14.

Penalties:
Gusev (tripping), 2:07; Soviet Bench Minor (served by Zimin), 4:13; Bergman (tripping), 15:16; Liapkin (slashing), 19:54; Kharlamov (10-minute misconduct), 19:54.

THIRD PERIOD
2. Canada - Cournoyer (Park) (PPG, GWG) 1:19.
3. USSR - Yakushev (Liapkin, Zimin) (PPG) 5:53.
4. Canada - P. Mahovlich (P. Esposito) (SHG) 6:47.
5. Canada - F. Mahovlich (Mikita, Cournoyer) 8:59.

Penalties:
Clarke (slashing), 5:15; Stapleton (hooking), 6:14.

Shots on goal				
	1	2	3	Total
USSR	7	5	9	21
Canada	10	16	10	36
Game MVPs				
USSR	Tretiak			
Canada	T. Esposito and P. Esposito			

Game 3
WINNIPEG   **September 6, 1972**

USSR 4   Canada 4

PLAYERS ON ICE:
Canada: Bergman, Stapleton, Park, Ellis, P. Esposito, Cournoyer, Cashman, White, Ratelle, Henderson, P. Mahovlich, Mikita, Parise, Savard, Lapointe, F. Mahovlich, Clarke

USSR: Gusev, Lutchenko, Kuzkin, Vasiliev, Tsygankov, Maltsev, Mishakov, Mikhailov, Shatalov, Yakushev, Petrov, Kharlamov, Shadrin, Solodukhin, Anisin, Lebedev, Bodunov

GOALIES:
Canada: T. Esposito
USSR: Tretiak

FIRST PERIOD
1. Canada - Parise (White, P. Esposito) 1:54.
2. USSR - Petrov (unassisted) (SHG) 3:16.
3. Canada - Ratelle (Cournoyer, Bergman) 18:25.

Penalties:
Vasiliev (elbowing), 3:02; Cashman (slashing), 8:01; Parise (tripping), 15:47.

SECOND PERIOD

4. Canada - P. Esposito (Cashman, Parise) 4:19.
5. USSR - Kharlamov (Tsygankov) (SHG) 12:56.
6. Canada - Henderson (Ellis, Clarke) 13:47.
7. USSR - Lebedev (Vasiliev, Anisin) 14:59.
8. USSR - Bodunov (Anisin) 18:28.

Penalties:
Petrov (interference), 4:46; Lebedev (tripping), 11:00.

THIRD PERIOD

No Scoring

Penalties:
White (slashing), 1:33; Mishakov (slashing), 1:33;
Cashman (slashing, misconduct), 10:44.

Shots on goal				
	1	2	3	Total
USSR	9	8	8	25
Canada	15	16	6	3
Game MVPs				
USSR	Tretiak			
Canada	Henderson			

Game 4
VANCOUVER   **September 8, 1972**

USSR 5   Canada 3

PLAYERS ON ICE:
Canada: Bergman, Stapleton, Park, Ellis, P. Esposito, Gilbert, Goldsworthy, D. Hull, Hadfield, Cournoyer, Seiling, White, Henderson, Awrey, F. Mahovlich, Clarke, Perreault

USSR: Lutchenko, Kuzkin, Ragulin, Vasiliev, Tsygankov, Blinov, Maltsev, Mikhailov, Yakushev, Petrov, Kharlamov, Vikulov, Shadrin, Anisin, Lebedev, Bodunov, Paladiev

GOALIES:
Canada: Dryden
USSR: Tretiak

FIRST PERIOD
1. USSR - Mikhailov, (Lutchenko, Petrov) (PPG) 2:01.
2. USSR - Mikhailov, (Lutchenko, Petrov) (PPG) 7:29.

Penalties:
Goldsworthy (crosschecking), 1:24; Goldsworthy (elbowing), 5:58; P. Esposito (tripping), 19:29.

SECOND PERIOD
3. Canada - Perreault, 5:37.
4. USSR - Blinov, (Petrov, Mikhailov) 6:34.
5. USSR - Vikulov, (Kharlamov, Maltsev) (GWG) 13:52.

Penalties:
Kuskin (tripping), 8:39.

THIRD PERIOD
6. Canada - Goldsworthy (Esposito, Bergman) 6:54.
7. USSR - Shadrin, (Yakushev, Vasiliev) 11:05.
8. Canada - Hull (P. Esposito, Goldsworthy) 19:38.

Penalties - Petrov (holding), 2:01.

Shots on goal				
	1	**2**	**3**	**Total**
USSR	11	4	6	21
Canada	10	8	23	41
Game MVPs				
USSR	Mikhailov			
Canada	P. Esposito			

Game 5

MOSCOW, USSR   **September 22, 1972**

Canada 4   **USSR 5**

PLAYERS ON ICE:

Canada: Bergman, Stapleton, Park, Ellis, P. Esposito, Gilbert, Cournoyer, Seiling, White, Ratelle, Henderson, P. Mahovlich, Parise, Lapointe, F. Mahovlich, Clarke, Perreault

USSR: Gusev, Lutchenko, Kuzkin, Ragulin, Tsygankov, Blinov, Maltsev, Mishakov, Mikhailov, Yakushev, Petrov, Kharlamov, Vikulov, Shadrin, Anisin, Liapkin, Martyniuk

GOALIES:

Canada: T. Esposito
USSR: Tretiak

FIRST PERIOD

1. Canada - Parise (Perreault, Gilbert) 15:30.

Penalties:

Ellis (tripping), 3:49; Kharlamov (slashing), 12:25.

SECOND PERIOD
2. Canada - Clarke (Henderson) 2:36.
3. Canada - Henderson (Lapointe, Clarke) 11:47.

Penalties:
Ellis (slashing), 5:38; Kharlamov (holding), 5:38;
Bergman (roughing), 8:13; Blinov (slashing), 20:00;
White (slashing), 20:00.

THIRD PERIOD
4. USSR - Blinov (Petrov, Kuzkin) 3:34.
5. Canada- Henderson (Clarke) 4:56.
6. USSR - Anisin (Liapkin, Yakushev) 9:05.
7. USSR - Shadrin (Anisin) 9:13.
8. USSR - Gusev, (Ragulin, Kharlamov) 11:41.
9. USSR - Vikulov (Kharlamov) (GWG) 14:46.

Penalties:
Clarke (holding), 10:25; Tsygankov (highsticking), 10:25;
Yakushev (hooking), 15:48.

Shots on goal				
	1	2	3	Total
Canada	12	13	13	37
USSR	9	13	11	33

Game MVPs	
Canada	T. Esposito, Henderson
USSR	Petrov, Yakushev

Game 6
MOSCOW **September 24, 1972**

Canada 3 USSR 2

PLAYERS ON ICE:
Canada: Bergman, Stapleton, Park, Ellis, P. Esposito, Gilbert, D. Hull, Cournoyer, Berenson, White, Ratelle, Henderson, P. Mahovlich, Parise, Savard, Lapointe, Clarke

USSR: Lutchenko, Ragulin, Vasiliev, Tsygankov, Maltsev, Mikhailov, Shatalov, Yakushev, Petrov, Kharlamov, Vikulov, Shadrin, Anisin, Lebedev, Bodunov, Liapkin, Volchkov

GOALIES:
Canada: Dryden
USSR: Tretiak

FIRST PERIOD
No Scoring.

Penalties:
Bergman (tripping), 10:21; P. Esposito (double-minor, charging), 13:11.

SECOND PERIOD
1. USSR - Liapkin (Yakushev, Shadrin) 1:12.
2. Canada - Hull (Gilbert) 5:13.
3. Canada - Cournoyer (Berenson) 6:21.
4. Canada- Henderson (unassisted) (GWG) 6:36.
5. USSR - Yakushev (Shadrin, Liapkin) (PPG) 17:11.

Penalties:
Ragulin (interference), 2:09; Lapointe (roughing), 8:29; Vasiliev (roughing), 8:29; Clarke (slashing, misconduct), 10:12; Hull (slashing), 17:02; P. Esposito (highsticking major), 17:46; Team Canada bench minor, 17:46.

THIRD PERIOD
No Scoring.

Penalties:
Ellis (holding), 17:39.

Shots on goal				
	1	2	3	Total
Canada	9	7	9	25
USSR	6	13	12	31
Game MVPs				
Canada	Dryden, Bergman			
USSR	Lutchenko, Yakushev			

Jim Prime

Game 7
MOSCOW   **September 26, 1972**

Canada 4   USSR 3

PLAYERS ON ICE:
Canada: Bergman, Stapleton, Park, Ellis, P. Esposito, Gilbert, Goldsworthy, D. Hull, Cournoyer, White, Ratelle, Henderson, P. Mahovlich, Parise, Savard, Lapointe, Clarke
USSR: Gusev, Lutchenko, Kuzkin, Ragulin, Vasiliev, Tsygankov, Blinov, Maltsev, Mishakov, Mikhailov, Yakushev, Petrov, Vikulov, Shadrin, Anisin, Liapkin, Volchkov

GOALIES:
Canada: T. Esposito
USSR: Tretiak

FIRST PERIOD
1. Canada - P. Esposito (Ellis, Henderson) 4:09.
2. USSR - Yakushev (Shadrin, Liapkin) 10:17.
3. USSR - Petrov (Vikulov, Tsygankov) (PPG) 16:27.
4. Canada- P. Esposito (Savard, Parise) 17:34.
Penalties:
Mikhailov (tripping), 2:00; P. Mahovlich (roughing), 5:16; Mishakov (holding), 5:16; Mishakov (holding), 11:09; P. Esposito (crosschecking), 12:39; White (interference), 15:45.

SECOND PERIOD
No Scoring.

Penalties:
Gilbert (hooking), 0:59; Parise (slashing), 6:04; Anisin (hooking), 6:11; P. Esposito (roughing), 12:44; Kuzkin (roughing), 12:44; Parise (roughing), 15:14; Kuzkin (roughing), 15:14; Stapleton (holding), 15:24.

THIRD PERIOD
5. Canada - Gilbert (Ratelle, Hull) 2:13.
6. USSR - Yakushev (Maltsev, Lutchenko) (PPG) 5:15.
7. Canada - Henderson (Savard) (GWG) 17:54.

Penalties:
Bergman (holding), 3:26; Gilbert (charging), 7:25; Bergman (roughing major), 16:26; Mikhailov (roughing major), 16:26.

Shots on goal	1	2	3	Total
Canada	7	8	7	22
USSR	12	8	9	29

Game MVPs	
Canada	P. Esposito, White
USSR	Mikhailov, Yakushev

Game 8
MOSCOW　　　　　**September 28, 1972**

Canada 6　　　USSR 5

PLAYERS ON ICE:
Canada: Bergman, Stapleton, Park, Ellis, P. Esposito, Gilbert, D. Hull, Cournoyer, White, Ratelle, Henderson, P. Mahovlich, Parise, Savard, Lapointe, F. Mahovlich, Clarke
USSR: Gusev, Lutchenko, Kuzkin, Vasiliev, Tsygankov, Blinov, Maltsev, Mishakov, Mikhailov, Yakushev, Petrov, Kharlamov, Vikulov, Shadrin, Anisin, Liapkin, Volchkov
GOALIES:
Canada:　　　Dryden
USSR:　　　Tretiak

FIRST PERIOD
1. USSR - Yakushev (Maltsev, Liapkin) (PPG) 3:34.
2. Canada - P. Esposito (Park) (PPG) 6:45.
3. USSR - Lutchenko (Kharlamov) (PPG) 13:10.
4. Canada - Park (Ratelle, Hull) 16:59.
Penalties:
White (holding), 2:25; P. Mahovlich (holding), 3:01; Petrov (hooking), 3:44; Parise (interference, misconduct, game misconduct), 4:10; Tsygankov (interference), 6:28; Ellis (interference), 9:27; Petrov (interference), 9:46; Cournoyer (interference), 12:51.

SECOND PERIOD

5. USSR - Shadrin (unassisted) 0:21.
6. Canada - White (Gilbert, Ratelle) 10:32.
7. USSR - Yakushev (unassisted) 11:43.
8. USSR - Vasiliev (unassisted) (PPG) 16:44.

Penalties:
Stapleton (crosschecking), 15:58; Kuzkin (elbowing), 18:06.

THIRD PERIOD

9. Canada - P. Esposito (P. Mahovlich) 2:27.
10. Canada - Cournoyer (P. Esposito, Park) 12:56.
11. Canada- Henderson (P. Esposito) (GWG) 19:26.

Penalties:
Gilbert (fighting major), 3:41; Mishakov (fighting major), 3:41; Vasiliev (tripping), 4:27; Hull (highsticking), 15:24; Petrov (elbowing), 15:24.

Shots on goal				
	1	2	3	Total
Canada	14	8	14	36
USSR	12	10	5	27
Game MVPs				
Canada	Henderson, Park			
USSR	Shadrin, Yakushev			

The Canadian Mint brought out a special toonie for the 50th anniversary of the Summit Series

Acknowledgements

The author would like to thank the following people, without whom this book could not have been published:

Andrew Wetmore—tenacious left winger who, like Paul Henderson, scored a winner in the last minute of play
Matt Clairmont—perennial assist leader and straight shooter
Glenna Prime—left- handed, left wing wife and coach
Catherine Prime—talented artist who always "wins the draw"
Ron Ellis—an unselfish, never-say-die team player. What hockey should be all about.
Paul Henderson—one of life's winners
Serge Savard—"a good person" and a good guy
Bobby Clarke—tough guy; honest man
Jeff, Jung, Margaret, Dave, Fin, Sam—a strong bench
Brenda Thompson—unflappable owner

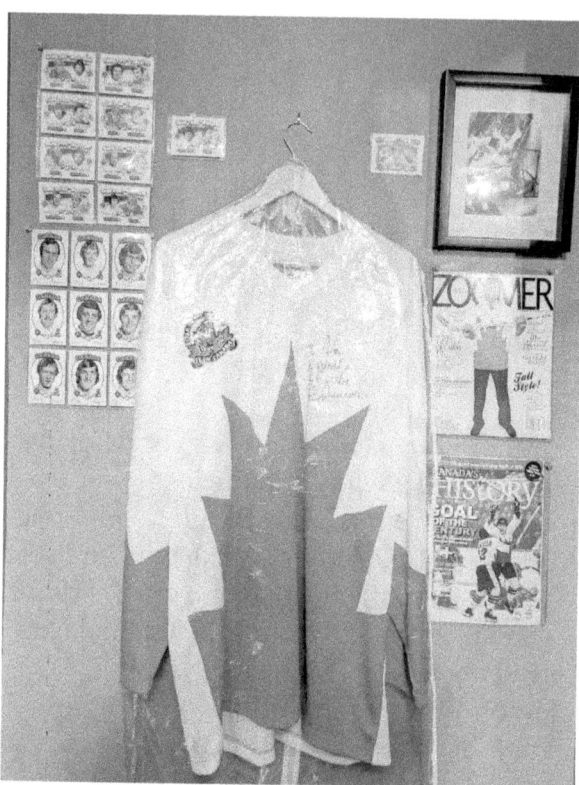

*The author's mementos of the Summit Series
include a jersey autographed by
Paul Henderson*

About the author

Jim Prime is the author of over 20 books, mostly on the subject of sports. He co-authored *Ted Williams' Hit List* with the legendary Boston Red Sox hitter and *How Hockey Explains Canada* with Canadian hockey icon Paul Henderson. He has also collaborated with baseball eccentric Bill "Spaceman" Lee on two books. He has contributed articles to various magazines including *Baseball Digest, Atlantic Insight, Atlantic Advocate, The Ring, Boxing Illustrated,* and the *Acadia Alumni Bulletin,* where he briefly served as editor. He's a five-time  winner of the People's Choice award at the Kings Shorts Festival of Ten Minute Plays in Annapolis Royal.

Jim grew up in Freeport on Long Island and will always consider himself an islander. He lives in New Minas in the Annapolis Valley with his wife, Glenna.

www.ingramcontent.com/pod-product-compliance
Lightning Source LLC
Chambersburg PA
CBHW081336120626
46546CB00011B/3366